SNIPPETS
OF SERBIA

Author: Emma Fick
Publisher: Komshe©2018 / info@komshe.com / www.komshe.com
Illustrations: Emma Fick
Design&Layout: Ivan Grujić

SNIPPETS
OF SERBIA

*illustrations
by emma fick*

dedication

for mama & papa
who both secure &
embolden me

and
for my brother Sam
who is unflinchingly
earnest & curious

TABLE of CONTENTS

introduction

When I first came to Serbia to teach English, I brought along my emergency art kit: one spiral-bound sketchbook, one set of black and colored pens, and a watercolor palette accompanied by a single brush. I hadn't touched paintbrush to paper in years— art had taken a back seat to academics during my college years—but I knew myself well enough to know I should always bring some art supplies along. Just in case.

As it happened, this *just-in-case* emergency kit provided exactly the tools I most needed—spiritually, intellectually, and creatively— to understand Serbia's complex intertwining narratives. Serbia is fascinating and baffling, captivating and frustrating, vibrant and confounding. There is no singularity to Serbian culture, and its historical, religious, cultural, culinary, and philosophical narratives are knots that must be carefully detangled.

And so illustration became my primary means of absorbing, synthesizing, and communicating Serbia. Contours, colors, a few lines of text: these exercises in condensed expression seemed to me to convey more than broad, sweeping generalizations about Serbian culture. The fuller scope of meaning, the truer significance of daily life was to be found in the string of peppers in the window, the intricacies of serving coffee, the soil-rimmed fingernails of a friend's grandmother.

Snippets are small pieces of things. They are people observed, foods consumed, ornaments spotted: a man on a bench, a small chocolate in foil, a floral border on a windowpane. They are conversations overheard and glimpses from bus windows. Strangers and friends, feelings and abstractions. Snippets are fragments that add up to a more holistic narrative.

This account is flawed and incomplete in the way all travels are flawed and incomplete: there are always landscapes left to see, flavors left to try, stories left to hear. I made assumptions and misunderstood words. My personal Serbian truth is not an empirical Serbian truth (if such a thing exists).

May these pages communicate the Serbia I know, and may you weave your own Serbian truth between the pages.

my FAMILY HISTORY

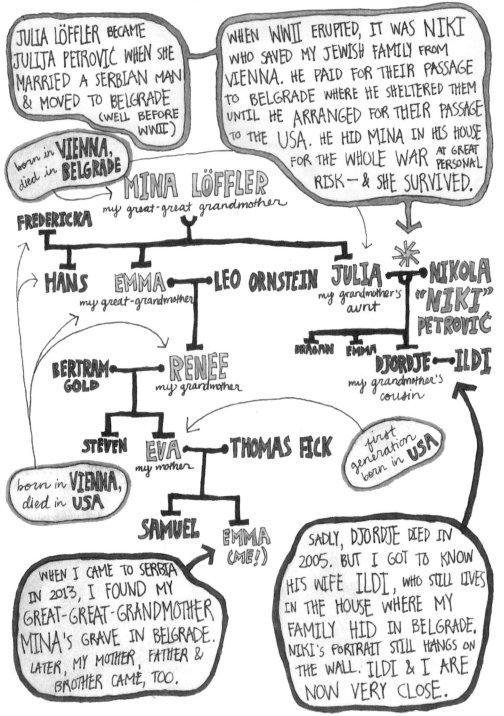

JULIA LÖFFLER BECAME JULIJA PETROVIĆ WHEN SHE MARRIED A SERBIAN MAN & MOVED TO BELGRADE (WELL BEFORE WWII)

WHEN WWII ERUPTED, IT WAS NIKI WHO SAVED MY JEWISH FAMILY FROM VIENNA. HE PAID FOR THEIR PASSAGE TO BELGRADE WHERE HE SHELTERED THEM UNTIL HE ARRANGED FOR THEIR PASSAGE TO THE USA. HE HID MINA IN HIS HOUSE FOR THE WHOLE WAR AT GREAT PERSONAL RISK — & SHE SURVIVED.

born in VIENNA, died in BELGRADE

MINA LÖFFLER
my great-great grandmother

FREDERICKA

HANS

EMMA — LEO ORNSTEIN
my great-grandmother

JULIA — NIKOLA "NIKI" PETROVIĆ
my grandmother's aunt

DRAGAN   EMMA

DJORDJE — ILDI
my grandmother's cousin

BERTRAM GOLD — RENEE
my grandmother

STEVEN   EVA — THOMAS FICK
my mother

first generation born in USA

born in VIENNA, died in USA

SAMUEL   EMMA (ME!)

WHEN I CAME TO SERBIA IN 2013, I FOUND MY GREAT-GREAT-GRANDMOTHER MINA'S GRAVE IN BELGRADE. LATER, MY MOTHER, FATHER & BROTHER CAME, TOO.

SADLY, DJORDJE DIED IN 2005. BUT I GOT TO KNOW HIS WIFE ILDI, WHO STILL LIVES IN THE HOUSE WHERE MY FAMILY HID IN BELGRADE. NIKI'S PORTRAIT STILL HANGS ON THE WALL. ILDI & I ARE NOW VERY CLOSE.

here's how it happened

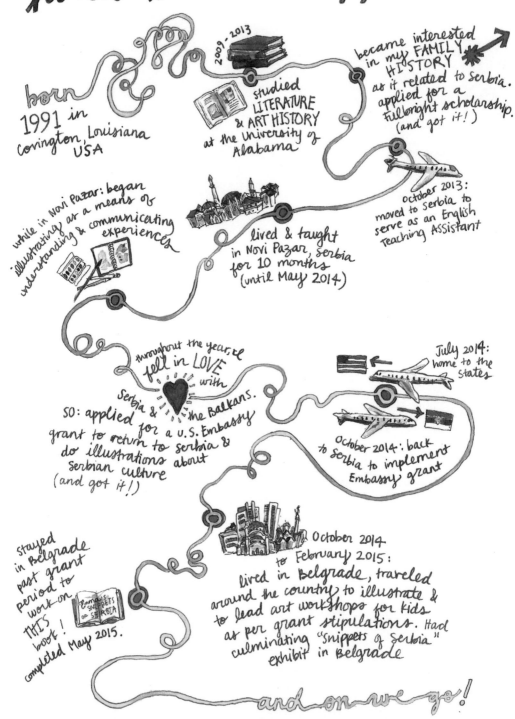

born 1991 in Covington, Louisiana USA

2009 - 2013 studied **LITERATURE & ART HISTORY** at the University of Alabama

became interested in my **FAMILY HISTORY** as it related to Serbia. applied for a Fulbright scholarship. (and got it!)

October 2013: moved to Serbia to serve as an English Teaching Assistant

lived & taught in Novi Pazar, Serbia for 10 months (until May 2014)

while in Novi Pazar: began illustrating as a means of understanding & communicating experiences

throughout the year, I fell in **LOVE** with Serbia & the Balkans. SO: applied for a U.S. Embassy grant to return to Serbia & do illustrations about Serbian culture (and got it!)

July 2014: home to the States

October 2014: back to Serbia to implement Embassy grant

October 2014 to February 2015: lived in Belgrade, traveled around the country to illustrate & to lead art workshops for kids as per grant stipulations. Had culminating "snippets of Serbia" exhibit in Belgrade

stayed in Belgrade past grant period to work on THIS book! completed May 2015.

Emma's SNIPPETS of SERBIA

and on we go!

SERBIA

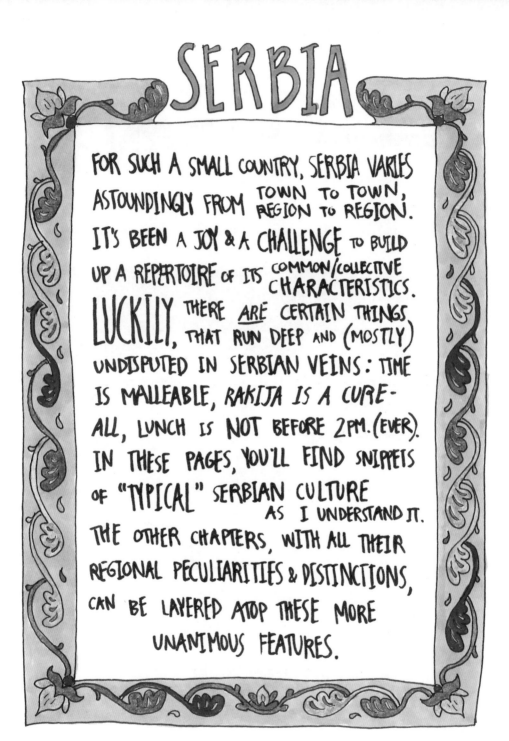

FOR SUCH A SMALL COUNTRY, SERBIA VARIES ASTOUNDINGLY FROM TOWN TO TOWN, REGION TO REGION. IT'S BEEN A JOY & A CHALLENGE TO BUILD UP A REPERTOIRE OF ITS COMMON/COLLECTIVE CHARACTERISTICS. LUCKILY, THERE _ARE_ CERTAIN THINGS THAT RUN DEEP AND (MOSTLY) UNDISPUTED IN SERBIAN VEINS: TIME IS MALLEABLE, _RAKIJA IS A CURE-ALL_, LUNCH IS NOT BEFORE 2PM. (EVER). IN THESE PAGES, YOU'LL FIND SNIPPETS OF "TYPICAL" SERBIAN CULTURE AS I UNDERSTAND IT. THE OTHER CHAPTERS, WITH ALL THEIR REGIONAL PECULIARITIES & DISTINCTIONS, CAN BE LAYERED ATOP THESE MORE UNANIMOUS FEATURES.

here's an easy way to identify a KAFANA:

← tables filled with chain smoking men = another promising sign

LOOK FOR THE RED & WHITE CHECKERED CURTAINS (AND MAYBE CHECKERED TABLECLOTHS, TOO)

in a restaurant, cafe, or kafana, don't fret over a few holes in the tablecloths:

CIGARETTE BURNS ARE SERBIA'S SPECIAL STAMP OF AUTHENTICITY.

SERBIAN FOOD PYRAMID

IT IS VERY SIMPLE BECAUSE THERE ARE ONLY **THREE** FOOD GROUPS: **MEAT, DAIRY + BREAD.**

(but, oh, the possibilities are endless!)

I THINK **KARAÐORÐEVA** (the letter Ð = DJ)
ŠNICLA EPITOMIZES SERBIAN
CUISINE AT ITS FINEST. AND BY "FINEST"
I MEAN MOST ABSURDLY RICH + HEAVY.

← this is how it looks on the plate. maybe you can guess why it's nicknamed "the maiden's dream." oy vey...

CROSS-SECTION:

1 = KAJMAK
2 = VEAL OR PORK CUTLET
3 = BREADING, FRIED

AND served with fries on the side.

I TOLD JOVAN I WOULD BE BACK IN ONE HOUR. WHEN I RETURNED 3 HOURS LATER, HE DIDN'T BAT AN EYE, JUST REMARKED:

"OH, YOU MEANT A SERBIAN HOUR."

I had a good laugh over that one!

TO FUNCTION IN THE BALKANS, YOU NEED TO GET IN A DALI STATE OF MIND ABOUT TIME:

↑
HOW I <u>USED</u>
TO THINK.

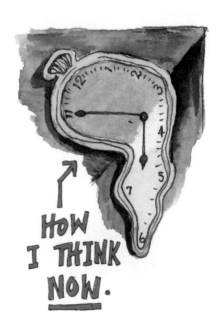

↑
HOW
I THINK
<u>NOW</u>.

Balkan time is more
fluid & imprecise.
Be flexible.

MEAL CONVENTIONS

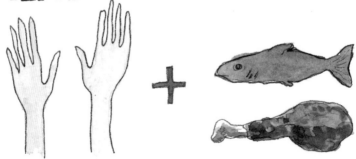

eat chicken & fish with your hands, but for other meats use a fork & knife.

 ← your bread goes on the table next to the plate, not ON the plate

BREAKFAST
optional

LUNCH
BIGGEST meal of the day!

DINNER
a small affair

8-10 AM   3 PM   9-10 PM

ALSO, IT'S NOT CONSIDERED A MEAL IF IT DOESN'T HAVE MEAT.

fish, fried
or baked

rice

beans

potato
salad

peppers
stuffed with beans

PRIME EXAMPLE: on
Christmas Eve, you "fast," which
means you eat things like: fish,
peppers stuffed with oily beans, lots
of potatoes, rice, salads, bread, nuts,
fruits, soups... only in Serbia could
such a feast be considered a FAST!

21

BEGINNER'S GUIDE TO
SERBIAN NECESSITIES

← you must have these ubiquitous mild cookies on hand AT ALL TIMES.

(I honestly think plazma® wrappers constitute 90% of litter in Serbia — look around!)

SMOKI, a puffy peanut-flavored snack ——→

NAJLEPŠE ŽELJE ("Best Wishes") chocolate — the required token gift for your hosts

← ZEBRA matches

VEGETA, the salty secret to most dishes

DEČIJI SAPUN (soap) & DR PAVLOVIĆ cream — the key to good skin for babies & adults alike →

In the market, remember:
PICK THE FLAWED FRUITS (& VEGGIES). THOSE
IMPERFECTIONS REVEAL THE FRUIT'S LOCAL,
NATURAL ORIGINS. YOU'LL GET A FAR
SUPERIOR FLAVOR, EVERY TIME.

bumps

bumps

spots

← YES.

NO. →

shiny

smooth,
perfect

THREE THINGS THAT GUARANTEE DEATH IN SERBIA

← **WET HAIR** even minor dampness is life-threatening if you set foot outside

DRAFT from cracked doors and windows, called **"PROMAJA."** Beware!

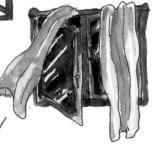

NO SOCKS- don't even <u>think</u> about it.

UNACCEPTABLE
BEHAVIOR:

PURSE

FLOOR

local lore says this will make you unlucky with money. You'll have strangers urging you to pick it up in an effort to rescue you from your unfortunate fate.

26

If I ask **ONE QUESTION** of **TWENTY PEOPLE,** I'll get **TWENTY DIFFERENT ANSWERS** of all shapes & sizes.

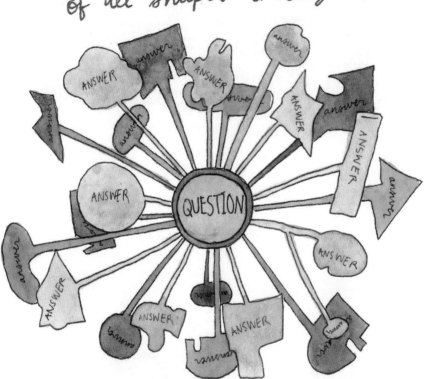

and, what's more: they'll **ALL BE TRUE** in their own way.

so many layers of understanding.

understanding
SERBIAN ORTHODOX CHRISTMAS

 Christmas day is on **JANUARY 7TH** because religious holidays go by the **JULIAN CALENDAR**

BEANS FISH POTATOES PASTA

Christmas Eve you **FAST**

Christmas Day you **FEAST**

ČESNICA SOUP SARMA PORK

WITHOUT meat or dairy

WITH meat + dairy

you decorate your home with

OAK BRANCHES

(more sparks mean more money in the coming year!)

on Christmas Eve, there's a huge fire at the church. Everyone gathers & adds their own branches to the fire

the growing wheat represents resurrection, new life, birth, etc.

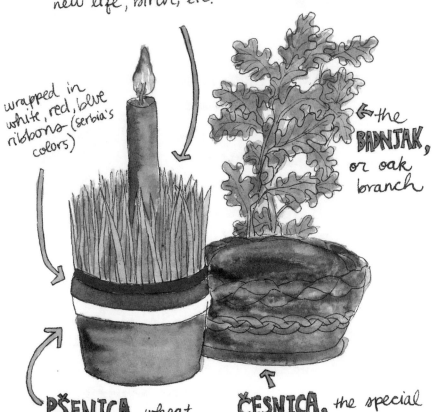

wrapped in white, red, blue ribbons (Serbia's colors)

← the **BADNJAK,** or oak branch

PŠENICA, wheat grass that was planted on St. Nikola's Day, December 19th

ČESNICA, the special Christmas bread. There's a coin hidden inside!

THE CHRISTMAS TABLE

understanding SLAVAS

↳ ST NIKOLA IS THE MOST COMMON

in Serbian Orthodoxy, each family has a patron saint. The saint is passed down, generation to generation, through the male line.

↳ ST NIKOLA'S DAY IS DECEMBER 19TH

each saint has his or her own day. The celebration on your family saint's day is called your **SLAVA**.

EACH YEAR ON YOUR FAMILY'S SLAVA, YOU HOST A DINNER— OR TWO, OR THREE — AND INVITE YOUR CLOSEST FRIENDS & FAMILY (WITH DIFFERENT SAINTS/SLAVAS) TO ATTEND.

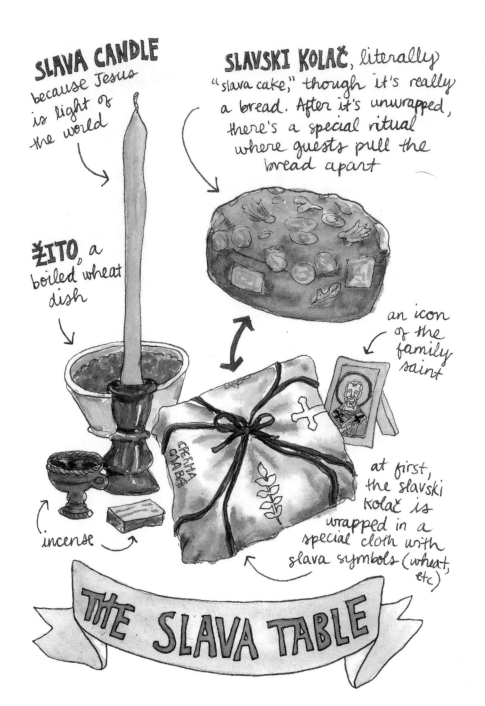

SLAVA CANDLE because Jesus is light of the world

SLAVSKI KOLAČ, literally "slava cake," though it's really a bread. After it's unwrapped, there's a special ritual where guests pull the bread apart

ŽITO, a boiled wheat dish

an icon of the family saint

at first, the slavski kolač is wrapped in a special cloth with slava symbols (wheat, etc)

incense

СРЕЋНА СЛАВА

THE SLAVA TABLE

31

MY FIRST SLAVA

potatoes

bread in various forms

TURSIJA, pickled veggies

Beans

savory pastries

TRLJANICA, pepper & leek salad

nuts

ajvar

rice

etc.

OKAY SO

NO ONE TOLD ME THIS WAS ONLY THE STARTER COURSE.

HUGE MISTAKE.

take fresh leaves & grasses; position them on raw eggs

wrap the eggs & leaves in socks or stockings. Tie tightly with string

fill big cooking pot with water & onion skins

(you've been saving those onion skins, RIGHT?)

let the eggs & onion skins boil on low heat for about an hour. Then, spoon the eggs out & let them cool.

the final (& best) part: unwrap the eggs & revel in their crimson splendor!

Orthodox Easter traditions

when someone says **"LET'S GET COFFEE"**, the word "COFFEE" can mean:

soda

beer

juice

rakija ← coffee

tea   wine →

BASICALLY, "COFFEE" IS A BLANKET TERM FOR ANYTHING IN LIQUID FORM
(IT EXPRESSES A DESIRE TO MEET; THE BEVERAGE ITSELF IS IRRELEVANT)

A COMPLETE GUIDE to DOMAĆA KAFA

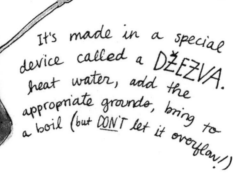

It's made in a special device called a DŽEZVA. heat water, add the appropriate grounds, bring to a boil (but <u>DON'T</u> let it overflow!)

pour coffee into small cups (without straining out the grounds). serve with sugar cubes or a jar of sugar — or, better yet, <u>BOTH</u>!

(NO MILK goes in domaća kafa)

DRINK UP! ENJOY!
note: BEWARE THE FINAL SIP. it's the grounds — coffee drudge — avoid the grainy-bitter mouthful at all costs.

MEET YOUR ALL-PURPOSE FRIENDS:
THE LITTLE STAND-ALONE KIOSKS THAT PEPPER STREETS EVERYWHERE.

newspapers, magazines

loto cards, pens, pencils

bus cards

phone credit

snacks, drinks

gum, candy

tissues, batteries

cigarettes, matches, lighters

WHEN IN DOUBT, TRY a TRAFIKA.

ESSENTIAL STREET SNACKS

popcorn (KOKICE) all day every day. Mathematically: cheap + satisfying = yes _please_.

ice cream (SLADOLED) in its various forms: by the scoop, in coffee, as a bar

you MUST try the plazma® flavor!

ANYTHING from a bakery (PEKARA), but I'm fond of **devrek**, a sesame-seed-encrusted pretzel-esque thing

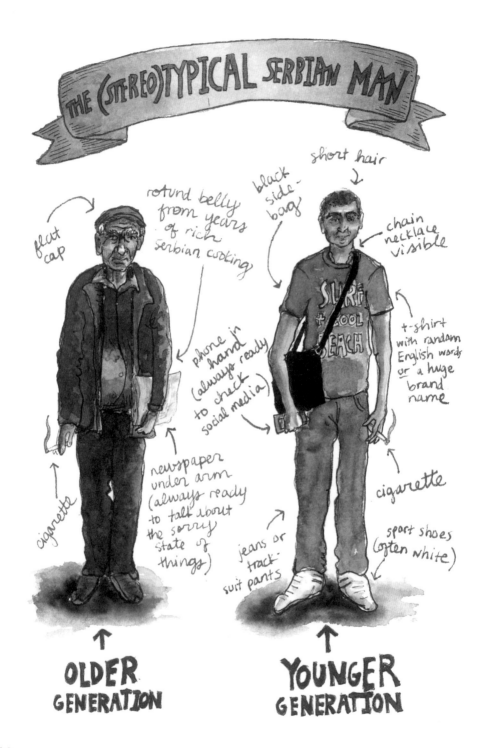

THE (STEREO)TYPICAL SERBIAN MAN

flat cap

rotund belly from years of rich Serbian cooking

black side-bag

short hair

chain necklace visible

phone in hand (always ready to check social media)

t-shirt with random English words or a huge brand name

cigarette

newspaper under arm (always ready to talk about the sorry state of things)

jeans or track-suit pants

cigarette

sport shoes (often white)

OLDER GENERATION

YOUNGER GENERATION

SMOKING SIGNS

these commonplace signs are so
funny to me. it's like they're proudly
proclaiming "SMOKE HERE, _PLEASE_."
Not only allowed, but also ENCOURAGED.
(did you know, serbia is the #1 country
in the world for per-capita cigarette
consumption?)

THE SERBIAN VERSION OF OBITUARIES:
PAPER CERTIFICATES POSTED AROUND TOWN. CERTAIN WALLS, OR DOORS, OR POLES, OR TREES BECOME UNOFFICIAL-OFFICIAL POSTING POINTS.

In one village, it was this lopsided, twisting tree

called "UMRLICA"

JOVAN JOVANOVIC
1921 - 2015

though the practice is best preserved in towns & villages, it still exists in cities as well. in Belgrade I spot it often in residential apartment complexes.

Orthodox Church norms

cross yourself before entering (forehead - navel - right shoulder - left shoulder). Some people also pause to kiss the door frame

kissing in general is a big part of the ritual — visit & kiss each icon (I love finding lip marks on the glass!). leave some money if you're so inspired

buy & light candles for your loved ones. each candle is a kind of prayer for the person — upper part is for living souls, lower part is for the dead.

RAKIJA 101

(pronounced RAH-kee-yah)

KAJSIJA, or apricot

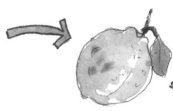

DUNJA, or quince

THE NATIONAL SERBIAN DRINK,
a kind of fruit brandy. Common flavors include

MEDOVAČA or honey (caution: VERY sweet)

KRUŠKA, or pear

ŠLJIVOVICA, or plum. the classic.

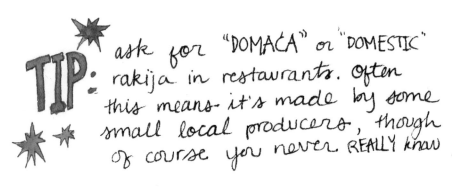

TIP: ask for "DOMAĆA" or "DOMESTIC" rakija in restaurants. Often this means it's made by some small local producers, though of course you never REALLY know

TRADITIONAL RAKIJA GLASSES, CALLED **ČOKANJČIĆ**. THE NARROW NECK PREVENTS SPILLAGE.

CLINK GLASSES, LOCK EYES & SAY "ŽIVELI!"

NOTE: YOU <u>SIP</u> RAKIJA, YOU DON'T THROW IT BACK LIKE A SHOT.

KAJMAK

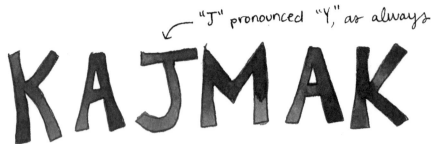

start with milk

heat it over low heat for a few hours

DEVOUR!

collect it & allow it to ferment

let it cool, then skim off the top layer of milk fat

FOR NEWBIES

closest equivalent is butter or clotted cream

IN THE PEKARA (BAKERY): a brief guide to Serbian Breads

POGAČA, your basic fluffy white bread, easily pulled apart into individual portions

LEPINJA/SOMUN a lovely tasty flatbread, hollow inside (easily stuff-able!)

← KIFLE crescent-shaped, often stuffed with cheese ("sa sirom")

← DJEVREK, boiled dough with sesame

PROJA serbian cornbread

POGAČICA →

(LISTEN, IF ALL MY DRAWINGS LOOK LIKE BEIGE LUMPS, IT'S BECAUSE THAT'S WHAT BREAD LOOKS LIKE, DANG-IT!)

HOW TO ROLL SARMA

place mound of
rice-meat-and-spice mixture
on bottom center of cabbage
leaf

fold over one
edge of the
leaf

start rolling (tightly!)
from the bottom... → all the way
to the end.

use
thumb
to tuck in the
loose end

arrange in pot
with bits of meat
between rolls

a catalogue of cures

for **BRUISES**, press cabbage leaves (or bread) on top

as a general rule, **RAKIJA** CURES **EVERYTHING.** for **SORE THROAT**, put a cloth soaked in rakija on your neck (and, as always, take a shot or two for good measure)

for **HEADACHE**, chop up a potato & wrap the slices around your forehead.

ROASTED PEPPERS,

STEP 1: place peppers on hot stove burner. Turn periodically until skins are completely black. Let cool.

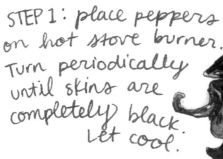

STEP 2: scrape/ peel off the burnt outer layer.

STEP 3: add oil, vinegar, salt & minced garlic. Toss, serve.

(yummm)

SERBIA - STYLE

SLATKO

a sweet fruit preserve — the word "slatko" literally means "sweet" — in which the fruits are kept whole in syrup.

traditionally, it's served to guests with a glass of water. Take one nibble, one sip, and say "MMM"

FOR DUMMIES*

* NOTE: <u>NOT</u> TO BE EATEN ON BREAD LIKE JAM. (NOT IN FRONT OF LOCALS, ANYWAY — BUT <u>THIS</u> GUILTY PARTY WON'T TELL A SOUL!)

Belgrade

I DON'T HAVE THAT MANY ILLUSTRATIONS ABOUT BELGRADE CONSIDERING HOW MUCH TIME I'VE SPENT HERE COMPARED TO OTHER PLACES IN SERBIA. I'M ALWAYS THINKING "I LIVE HERE; I CAN ILLUSTRATE THAT NEXT WEEK." WHICH MEANS MANY ILLUSTRATIONS ARE POST-PONED INTO OBLIVION. I RELISH THE ENDLESS ADVENTURE OF FINDING NEW CAFÉS, SIDE STREETS, TUCKED-AWAY COURTYARDS. BELGRADE IS MY SECOND HOME, AND IT'S NOT JUST A MATTER OF MONTHS SPENT HERE (8!). I'LL ALWAYS BE SENTIMENTAL ABOUT THESE STREETS: IN MY MIND, THEY'LL BE FOREVER TIED TO MY DEVELOPMENT AS AN ARTIST.

MY FAVORITE GRAFFITI ART IN THE SAVAMALA DISTRICT

maybe I'm just a sucker for puns.

the ever-changing
LEDGE OF CURIOSITIES
on Hilandarska street

↑

THE ASSORTMENT OF OBJECTS CHANGES EVERY DAY. NEVER FAILS TO MAKE ME SMILE.

imposing, imperious

SOCIALIST APARTMENT BLOCKS IN NEW BELGRADE.

wavy
blonde
hair

shiny
leather
jacket

some non-
descript guy
with a beer
belly (and,
probably,
a nice
car)

skin-tight
white
dress
(through
which
underwear
is clearly
visible)

snakeskin-
print purse

knee-
high
boots

familiar street scene,
Belgrade

ST SAVA CHURCH
in Belgrade

SURE, IT'S ENORMOUS, BUT ITS GAPING,
UNFINISHED INTERIOR STANDS IN STARK
CONTRAST TO ITS PRISTINE EXTERIOR.
IT'S BEEN UNDER CONSTRUCTION FOR OVER A CENTURY!

public TRANSPORT PORTRAITS

elegance on Bus 37,
Belgrade, 1:30pm.

MORNING SNACK AMONG THE APPLES.

apple vendor, Belgrade

'TIS THE SEASON

strings of dried peppers hanging in the window, preparing for winter.

"the house with the green tiles"

ONE OF THE FINEST EXAMPLES OF SECESSION (ART NOUVEAU) ARCHITECTURE IN BELGRADE.

public TRANSPORT PORTRAITS

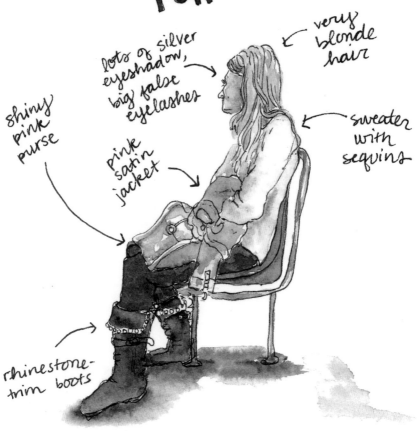

very blonde hair

lots of silver eyeshadow, big false eyelashes

shiny pink purse

sweater with sequins

pink satin jacket

rhinestone-trim boots

SO MUCH SPARKLE.
Belgrade, Tram 2, 8:45am.

the flower sellers

(and some → potatoes for good measure)

ROW OF KITTIES,
WAITING OH-SO
HOPEFULLY &
PATIENTLY

OUTSIDE
THE FISH
SHOP.

(meows are an international auxiliary language.)

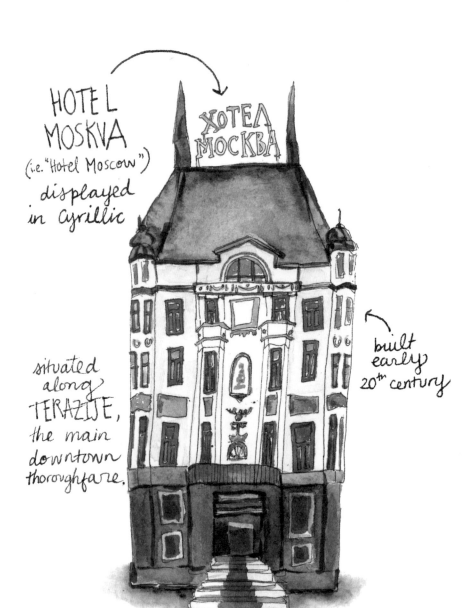

HOTEL
MOSKVA
(i.e. "Hotel Moscow")
displayed
in Cyrillic

ХОТЕЛ
МОСКВА

situated
along
TERAZIJE,
the main
downtown
thoroughfare.

built
early
20th century

AN ARCHITECTURAL LANDMARK IN BELGRADE.
I LIKE IT FOR ITS LANKY PROPORTIONS AND
POINTY TURRETS, WHICH GIVE IT AN AIR OF WHIMSY.

shoelace vendors

inexplicably, almost always ~~sold~~ with HAIR ACCESSORIES

← DIY contraption
for a shoe-shine

I FEEL LIKE, GIVEN THE QUANTITY OF THESE VENDORS, BELGRADE HAS FAR MORE SHOELACES THAN IT HAS PAIRS OF SHOES/FEET TO PUT THEM ON.

OCTOBER

SPOILS FROM THE MARKET, PART I

home-made REN, or horseradish sauce

AJVAR, extra ljuto (spicy)

← small apples

big figs

← pears

mushrooms, assorted

OCTOBER

SPOILS FROM THE MARKET, PART II

leeks

dill

dried chanterelle mushrooms

fig slatko

pumpkin seeds

sunflower seeds

pumpkin, pre-shredded

NOTE: LIST IS BY <u>NO</u> MEANS COMPREHENSIVE

socialist-style giants

mid-size, more modern apartment building

old-style houses constructed with wooden frames, wattle-and-daub exteriors, & red shingle roofs

THE VIEW FROM LJUBICA'S BALCONY ON VOJVODE ŠUPLJIKCA STREET. HAPHAZARD, LAYERED; A JUMBLE, NO COHESION. MICROCOSM: BELGRADE'S ESSENCE.

A DISCARDED GOLDEN ARMCHAIR, LOOKING REGAL BY THE DUMPSTER

on the street,
Belgrade

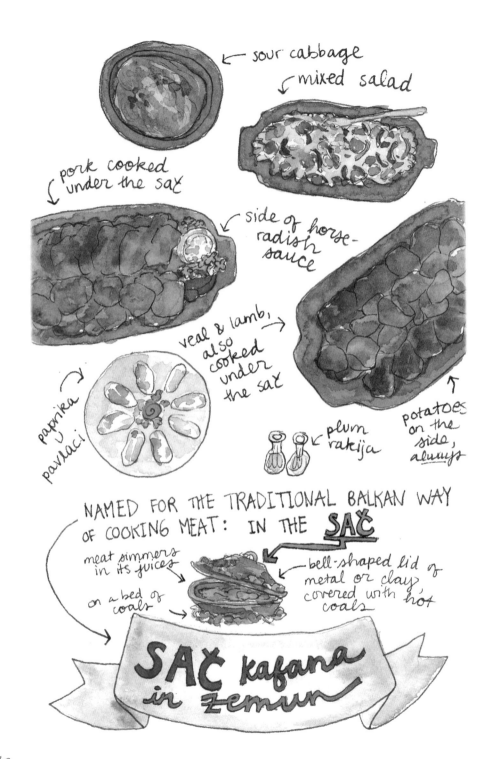

← sour cabbage

mixed salad

pork cooked under the sač

side of horse-radish sauce

veal & lamb, also cooked under the sač

paprika v pavlaci

plum rakija

potatoes on the side, always

NAMED FOR THE TRADITIONAL BALKAN WAY OF COOKING MEAT: IN THE **SAČ**

meat simmers in its juices

on a bed of coals

bell-shaped lid of metal or clay, covered with hot coals

SAČ kafana in zemun

public TRANSPORT PORTRAIT

tram 3, 3pm, Belgrade

BEHIND THE SCENES IN BELGRADE'S NATIONAL MUSEUM, WITH THE PRESIDENT of the STEERING COMMITTEE:

a Pissarro painting hanging casually in the office

(makes me think about what other gems must lie in wait!)

THE MUSEUM IS CONSTANTLY "UNDERGOING RENOVATIONS" AND STRAPPED FOR CASH. WHAT A SHAME! IT'S BEEN CLOSED SINCE 2002 (THOUGH IT DOES HOST TEMPORARY EXHIBITIONS).

climb up here for a spectacular view over Zemun

built in 1896 to cele-
brate 1,000 years of Hungarian habitation on the Pannonian plain.

GARDOŠ TOWER

EF 2014

ZEMUN

crumbling facades →

↑ cobbled streets

IF IT SEEMS LIKE A TOTALLY DIFFERENT CITY FROM BELGRADE, THAT'S BECAUSE IT *WAS* — UNTIL 1934. TODAY, THE NEIGHBORHOOD BOASTS RUSTIC CHARM, ITS CRUMBLING FACADES & COBBLED STREETS LEADING DOWN TO THE DANUBE WATERFRONT.

a shop in zemun

piles of scarves & other knitted/ woven goodies. can they ALL be mine?

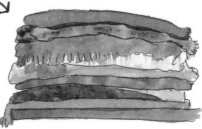

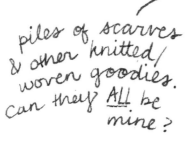

the loom sits in the middle of the shop

hoo-ray handicrafts

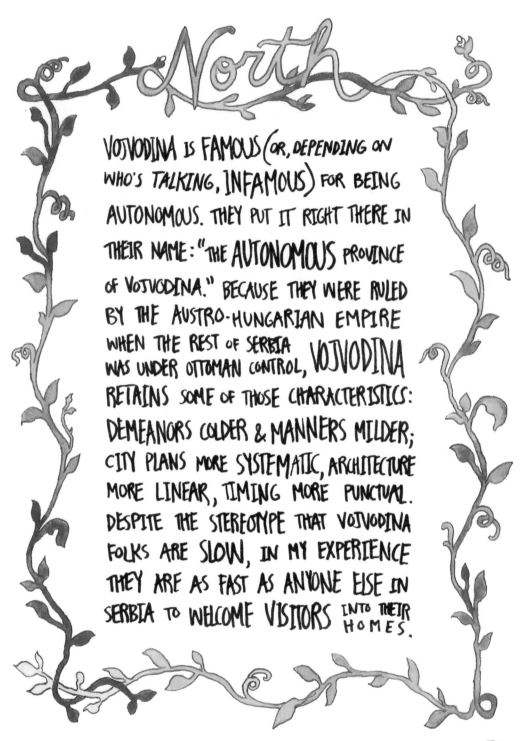

North

VOJVODINA IS FAMOUS (OR, DEPENDING ON WHO'S TALKING, INFAMOUS) FOR BEING AUTONOMOUS. THEY PUT IT RIGHT THERE IN THEIR NAME: "THE AUTONOMOUS PROVINCE OF VOJVODINA." BECAUSE THEY WERE RULED BY THE AUSTRO-HUNGARIAN EMPIRE WHEN THE REST OF SERBIA WAS UNDER OTTOMAN CONTROL, VOJVODINA RETAINS SOME OF THOSE CHARACTERISTICS: DEMEANORS COLDER & MANNERS MILDER; CITY PLANS MORE SYSTEMATIC, ARCHITECTURE MORE LINEAR, TIMING MORE PUNCTUAL. DESPITE THE STEREOTYPE THAT VOJVODINA FOLKS ARE SLOW, IN MY EXPERIENCE THEY ARE AS FAST AS ANYONE ELSE IN SERBIA TO WELCOME VISITORS INTO THEIR HOMES.

understanding VOJVODINA

VOJVODINA IS DISTINCT & PROUD OF IT — AS EVIDENCED BY THEIR ADDITION OF "*THE AUTONOMOUS* REGION" TO THEIR NAME.

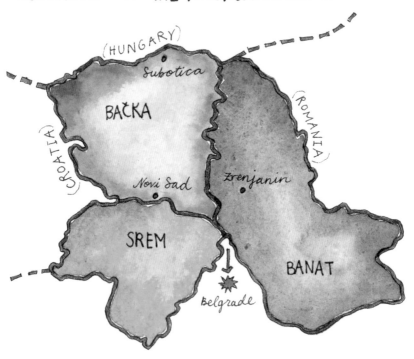

DIVIDED INTO 3 REGIONS: BAČKA, BANAT & SREM, ACCORDING TO SOCIOPOLITICAL/CULTURAL HERITAGE. NOVI SAD IS THE LARGEST CITY WITH 250,000 PEOPLE; SUBOTICA IS NEXT (100,000), FOLLOWED BY ZRENJANIN (75,000). SO YOU GET AN IDEA OF HOW RURAL THE MAJORITY OF VOJVODINA IS. GREAT EXPANSES OF FARM LAND.

VOJVODINA

all variety of doors

ZRENJANIN · NOVI SAD · SUBOTICA

TRG SLOBODE, the main square

the cathedral is the city's most central & recognizable landmark. Don't be surprised if someone asks to meet you there

wide, beautiful streets are conducive to strolling & relaxing (so THAT'S why people here move so slow...)

Novi Sad

passages

IT ALWAYS PAYS TO DUCK THROUGH THE
ALLEYS. OFTEN, AN ENTIRE MINI UNIVERSE
WILL BE REVEALED. LUSH OASES IN THE CITY CENTER

81

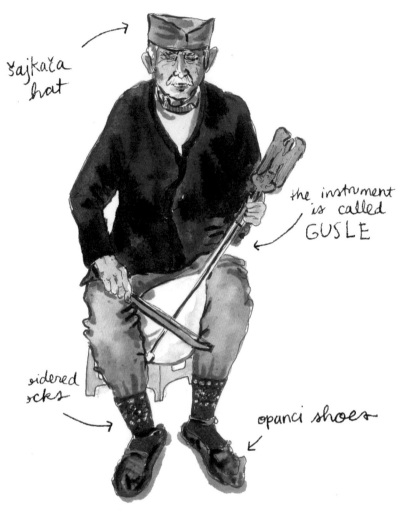

šajkača hat

the instrument
is called
GUSLE

oidered
ocks

opanci shoes

the street performer
NOVI SAD

THE CITY IS COLLECTIVELY PROUD OF ITS
TWO RESIDENT SWANS:

Elsa & Bisa

⌐ short for "Isidore"   ⌐ short for "Bisenija"

THEY LIVE IN DANUBE PARK. EVERY CHILD KNOWS &
LOVES THEM. THEY HAVE "ALWAYS" LIVED THERE—
PERMANENT FIXTURES OF THE NOVI SAD LANDSCAPE,
immortal

THE LIMAN
APARTMENT BLOCKS
ringing the historic city center —

divided into 4 socialist-era complexes. University students mostly live in Liman 1; the rest are general residential areas.

public TRANSPORT PORTRAITS

sheer exhaustion on the
train, Subotica to Belgrade

Subotica

THIS NORTHERN CITY PRESSES UP AGAINST HUNGARY

(built in 1904 & exploding with whimsy!)

IT'S PERHAPS BEST KNOWN FOR ITS ORNATE SECESSIONIST/ART NOUVEAU ARCHITECTURE.

Raichle Palace, for example

SUBOTICA'S STREET SIGNS ARE AN APT INDICATION OF THE CONFLUENCE OF CULTURES FOUND THERE:

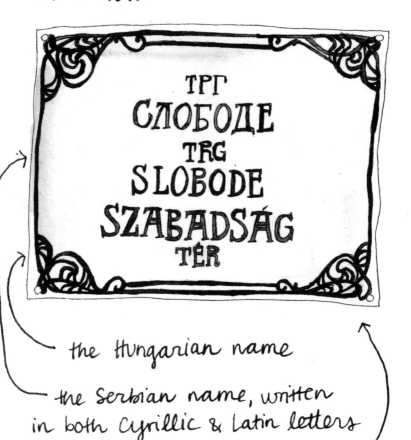

ТРГ
СЛОБОДЕ
TRG
SLOBODE
SZABADSÁG
TÉR

the Hungarian name

the Serbian name, written in both Cyrillic & Latin letters

and also, note the omnipresent art nouveau decorative elements — organic lines snaking across everything!

the Subotica synagogue

A MASTERPIECE — AND AN ANOMALY,
AS FAR AS SYNAGOGUES GO. a bit worse
for the wear, but undergoing renovation.

GOULASH FOR ONE,
intended for three.
I MADE A VALIANT EFFORT!

homemade pasta, noodles thick & flat, with crumbly cheese sprinkled atop

tender chunks of veal, thick & tasty sauce. spiced with bay leaves, etc

bread

spicy paprika

srpska salata

BATES RESTAURANT, SUBOTICA

ZRENJANIN

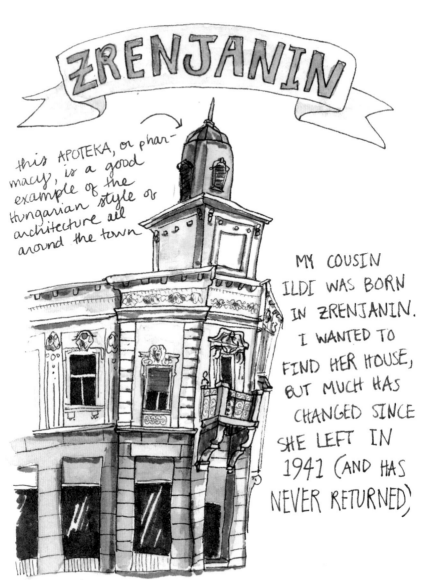

this APOTEKA, or pharmacy, is a good example of the Hungarian style of architecture all around the town

MY COUSIN ILDI WAS BORN IN ZRENJANIN. I WANTED TO FIND HER HOUSE, BUT MUCH HAS CHANGED SINCE SHE LEFT IN 1941 (AND HAS NEVER RETURNED)

she tried to give me directions to her house based on the location of the single pharmacy that was on the main street in 1941. Now there are a few. Though I didn't manage to find her house, I _did_ find "THE pharmacy." Close!

THIS IS AN ORIGINAL CITROEN 4 FROM
THE 1930s. IT'S SPECIAL BECAUSE IT'S
ALWAYS BEEN IN THE FAMILY: PASSED
DOWN THROUGH GENERATIONS, NEVER SOLD.

textile roof

wooden
steering
wheel →

well-loved, as
evidenced by the
gleaming exterior

ON THE STREET, ZRENJANIN

around the corner, on the side wall of the ornate town hall facade, I find wrinkled, deteriorating building-skin.

PAST SPLENDOR: A THIN VENEER OVER ITS CURRENT DISREPAIR.

example of a broader observed through out the (a small pattern city.)

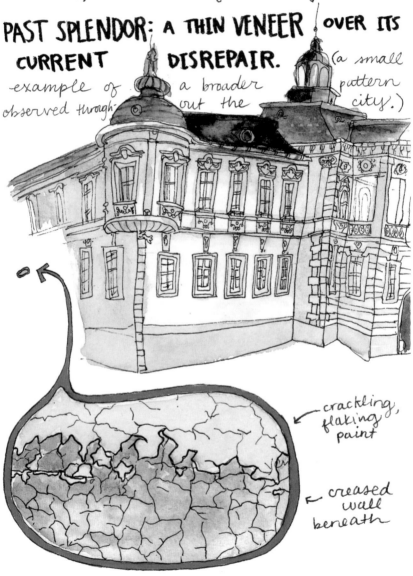

crackling, flaking paint

creased wall beneath

WALKING ALONG BEGEJ RIVER

fisherman with
a big square net

DVOLJNO PRODAJEM
PILIĆE

una dostava
dru adps
-kom
nkom

Telefon
023/88
060/08

UREDENI 250 din/kg

sign on a wooden
lamppost advertising with entrepreneurial
spirit: SELLING FARM CHICKENS FOR A GOOD
PRICE. HOME DELIVERIES ON TUESDAYS AND FRIDAYS.
evidently a successful business venture;
all but one of the phone numbers are <u>taken</u>!

STARA MORAVICA

all variety of doors

SREMSKI KARLOVCI

all variety of doors

STARA MORAVICA

A BUCOLIC HUNGARIAN VILLAGE IN VOJVODINA, THE NORTHERN REGION OF SERBIA. POPULATION: 6,000. LANGUAGE SPOKEN: HUNGARIAN (90% OF POPULATION). DATE FOUNDED: 1786. CHARM: UNEQUIVOCAL.

houses are often built in identical rows

it's traditional for Hungarian-style homes to have these flat facades & to display the year they were constructed here

Wide, straight streets, just BEGGING you to stroll down them

WE ARRIVED TO A FRESH LAYER OF SNOW OVER EVERYTHING.

KITCHENS ARE IMPORTANT

THIS ONE — WELL-EQUIPPED, COZY — APPROACHES PERFECTION!

the indispensable ——→
wood-burning stove,
making the air all warm
and toasty & filling the
room with its woodsy
fragrance.

WINE TASTING with Vili

HIS SMALL, UNASSUMING OPERATION YIELDS AWARD-WINNING PRODUCTS.

a generous spread of smoked meats, cheeses, & fresh-baked POGAČICA pastries, all flaky & lard-filled

wines are sold in repurposed 2-liter plastic bottles — now that's how you know it's legit!

WE WHILED AWAY THE AFTERNOON IN VILI'S COLD, DARK, ACRID-SMELLING, WOODEN-BARREL-FILLED CELLAR, SAMPLING HIS DELECTABLE WINES. FAVORITES INCLUDED: FRANKOVKA, PRIMUS, PINOT NOIR & SHIRAZ.

IT'S BEEN **DAMN** COLD — DOWN TO -20°C (-4°F)

no worries, though, because I received some excellent local advice on

HOW TO STAY WARM.

first, TAKE OFF YOUR HAT & PUT IT ON YOUR FEET.

then, START DRINKING.

brandy is always a good choice.

...**keep** **drinking**.

finally, WHEN ONE HAT TURNS INTO **TWO**... *you know you'll be alright.*

PAČIR

A VILLAGE NEAR—

AS IN, 5 KM (3 MILES) <u>NEAR</u> — STARA MORA-VICA. HALF SERBIAN, HALF HUNGARIAN. we went in search of cheese; BOY DID WE FIND IT — AND SO MUCH MORE! — WITH THE BENEFICENT SREDOJEVIĆ FAMILY.

← Dara, the matriarch & expert cheese maker

she's holding the wooden instrument she uses to churn butter

CHEESE!

their plum rakija

their special cherry wine — they even sent Tanja & me home with our own bottles!

3-tiered sweets platter, a giant cake

cheese pastries: one plate salty, one plate sweet

(everything homemade!)

AND ALL THIS BEFORE SAMPLING MOUNTAINS OF DARA'S DELICIOUS CHEESE

HOSPITALITY at the SREDOJEVIĆ HOME.

SOUTH

THE SOUTH GETS A BAD RAP IN SERBIA. THERE'S ONE SAYING THAT GOES "ŠTO JUŽNIJE, TO TUŽNIJE." *"THE MORE SOUTH, THE MORE SAD."* NOW, MAYBE IT'S BECAUSE I'M FROM THE SOUTH IN THE U.S. AND WE DEAL WITH MANY SIMILAR STEREOTYPES, BUT I GET DEFENSIVE WHEN I HEAR THAT. IT'S TRUE THAT SOUTHERN SERBIA IS MORE ECONOMICALLY DEPRESSED AND MORE RURAL. PEOPLE HAVE AN ACCENT. (ALL OF THESE THINGS PARALLEL THE AMERICAN SOUTH). BUT THE PEOPLE HAVE A SPECIAL SPIRIT, THE FOOD A DISTINCT FLAVOR, THE MUSIC A PARTICULAR SOUND. THE LANDSCAPE IS LOVELY. PLUS, I ATTENDED MY VERY FIRST SLAVA IN VRANJE, SO IT WILL ALWAYS HAVE A SPECIAL PLACE IN MY HEART.

NIŠ

NOTABLY, THE BIRTHPLACE OF BOTH :

Constantine the Great

first Christian emperor, established Roman Byzantine empire

lived circa 272 to 337 ACE

— AND —

Burek

the omnipresent (& omnidelicious) oily, salty, flaky Balkan pastry, filled with cheese or meat & chased down with sips of yogurt.

depending on whether I'm thinking with my STOMACH or my BRAIN ———→

(OF EQUAL HISTORICAL SIGNIFICANCE...?!)

no trip to Niš is complete without a grim visit to

THE SKULL TOWER.

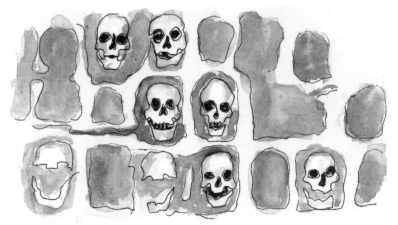

WHY, YES — YES IT _IS_ A TOWER BUILT of HUMAN HEADS.
YOU SHOULD LOOK IT UP.

- -

and now, for a macabre segueway:
SPEAKING of HEADS, THIS

IS A TRADITIONAL NIŠ HAT
(IT'S ALL WOOLLY!) FROM
DAYS OF YORE

IN NIŠ, I LIKE PLAYING "I SPY" WITH THE ROMAN BRICKS. THEY'VE BEEN THERE SINCE ANTIQUITY, REPURPOSED BY EACH POWER & EMPIRE THAT CAME AFTER.

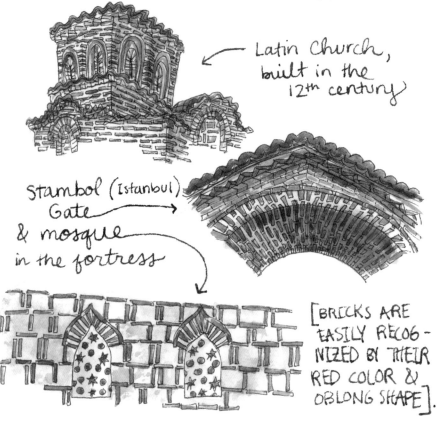

Latin Church, built in the 12th century

Stambol (Istanbul) Gate & mosque in the fortress

[BRICKS ARE EASILY RECOGNIZED BY THEIR RED COLOR & OBLONG SHAPE].

they are tangible portrayals of history's layering effect, how everything builds — literally, ideologically — on what came before.

REMNANTS OF ANCIENT PAGAN PRACTICES OBSERVED IN CURRENT ORTHODOX TRADITIONS.

apples ⟶

← rakija

⟵ doll

UNUSUAL ADDITIONS TO THE CLASSIC WEDDING BOWER. SPOTTED IN GORNJI MATEJEVAC VILLAGE.

one can see foods — especially apples — left in sacred places for dead souls to enjoy? A spillover from Slavic pagan roots.

apples, candies

rakija, oil, water

A COMMON SIGHT: EDIBLE OFFERINGS ON ICONS & ON GRAVES. SPOTTED IN LATIN CHURCH.

← LAMB SOUP

BELMUŽ, a regional cheese specialty ↳

KISELI KUPUS, or SOUR CABBAGE ↓

ROASTED LAMB + POTATOES ↓

my new favorite: **VEAL HEAD,** all cooked into a tender mush

MORAVSKA SALATA, named for the nearby river Morava. mix of tomato, pepper & garlic deliciousness.

BREAD ↗

lunch at NIŠLIJSKA MEHANA

IN SOUTHERN SERBIA —

Niš, Vranje, environs — THE OTTOMAN INFLUENCE LINGERS. it can be seen, for example, in the — **RATLUK,**

OR TURKISH DELIGHT, served alongside Turska Kafa (Turkish coffee) in almost every café.

VRANJE

FIRST THINGS FIRST:
FOOD.

SAMSA traditional breakfast: rolled layers of thin pastry dough, topped with garlicky yogurt

TRLJANICA SALATA a regional salad of peppers, chopped leeks, oil, salt, vinegar

CRVENCI a gelatinous dessert named for its red (crven) color. made of cornstarch, flour, sugar, raspberry extract.

TARANA a kind of meat lasagna, baked in a shallow pan under the coals. chicken or pork meat + kore (sheets of pastry dough) + tomato sauce.

man heading
home from
the market,

LEEKS
IN
TOW

on the street,
Vranje

TINY STONE CHURCH, 14TH CENTURY, PERCHED ATOP SPINDLY, STATUESQUE ROCK FORMATIONS.

freshly-dug pits beside the church — just one week previous, they discovered 14th-century skeletons here!

a friendly goat shepherd came to unlock the church for us. he told us he's psychic — that's how he knew we were visiting that day

camouflage vest

LOCAL VILLAGERS FEAR THAT THE CHURCH, NAMED PRESVETA BOGORODICA, IS POSSESSED BY EVIL SPIRITS DUE TO ITS SURROUNDINGS, WHICH ARE CALLED "DEVIL'S STONES."

generations in passing

ON THE STREET, VRANJE

AN AMUSING MODERN TAKE ON THE CLASSIC FOUNDER'S PORTRAIT: THE 1904 BENEFACTOR LOOKING AT A BLUEPRINT OF THE CHURCH, FINGERING HIS STACKS OF GOLD COINS WITH A VERY FORLORN EXPRESSION ON HIS FACE.

you can see that this brick portion (Roman bricks, again!) is much older than the rest of the church

Prohor Pcinjski

first founded in 11th century. renovated in 14th century & again in the 19th when the white part was added.

vranje array

THE WHITE BRIDGE,
built for two young lovers
who died tragically
for one another

radiating patterns
on the ceilings at
PASHA'S HOUSE

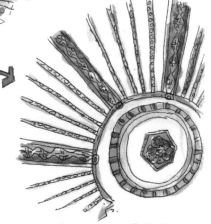

KOLUMBO KAFA,
OR "COLUMBUS COFFEE,"
Vranje's specific brand
of Turkish coffee. It's
always freshly ground &
has a famously strong flavor.

VRANJE: constantly under construction.

from my perspective, it looks to be a lot of observing/discussing piles of debris.

not so many attempts to actually move said debris.

SERBIAN SENSIBILITY EASILY EXPLAINS THAT THIS IS BE-CAUSE CONSTRUCTION PROJECTS BEGIN DURING ELEC-TIONS (promises! progress!) AND PROMPTLY END WHEN THE POLITICIAN TAKES OFFICE. BUT—NEVER FEAR! YOU ONLY HAVE TO WAIT FOR THE NEXT ELECTION FOR WORK TO RESUME...

Vranjska Banja

EVEN MORE THAN THE SPA CENTER ITSELF, **TWO THINGS** CAUGHT MY EYE:

FIRST, the enormous abandoned hotel "Jumkovic," lying in half-finished ruin since the early '80s.

and **SECOND,** how they prepared coffee for us, sans stove, in the small box of a tourism office: they brought an empty jug to the nearest hot spring, where water bubbled, naturally boiling, to the surface. Voila! Nescafé, spa-style!

with no reliable public transportation to tourist sites, it's hard to make it to a lot of monuments around these parts.

BUT, I **FINALLY** *made it to* **STUDENICA**

à la the 14th century fresco of King milutin, holding the church.

PAVLICA CHURCH
BUILT 12ᵀᴴ CENTURY

dangling precipitously over a small cliff!

STARA PAVLICA IS ABOUT 28 KM FROM NOVI PAZAR, OR 8KM FROM NEIGHBORING RAŠKA. PRIME EXAMPLE OF THE RAŠKA SCHOOL STYLE.

we enjoy
THE MANY FACETS
OF NOVI PAZAR

ST BOJAN AND HIS HOLY IRON MAIDEN

THAT TRUSTY OLD SET OF WHEELS
CONSTITUTES RELIGIOUS DEVOTION—
ALL HAIL YUGO!

121

IN NOVI PAZAR, EVERYONE BUYS THEIR COFFEE **FRESHLY-GROUND** IN ONE OF THESE SMALL (AND **DIVINE-SMELLING**) SHOPS.

whole coffee beans of your roast choice (light, medium or dark) are put here

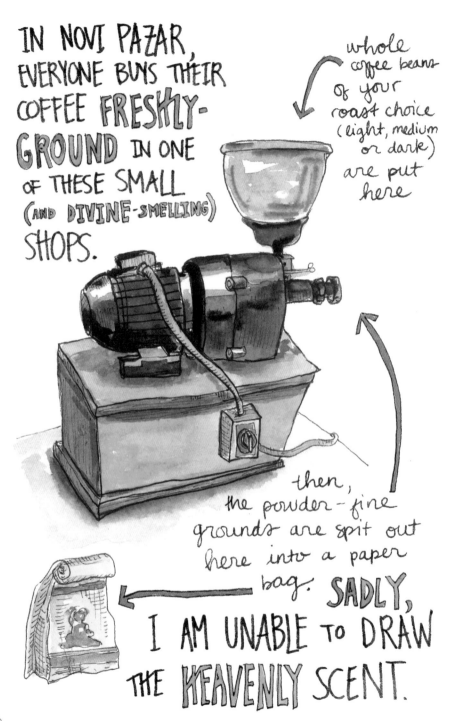

then, the powder-fine grounds are spit out here into a paper bag. **SADLY,** I AM UNABLE TO DRAW THE **HEAVENLY** SCENT.

ST PETER'S CHURCH

IN NOVI PAZAR IS THE <u>OLDEST</u> IN SERBIA.

most was built in the 9th century, but its foundations are much older

I love how it looks a little lopsided

INSIDE, YOU CAN CLIMB UP TO A CAVE-LIKE GALLERY WHERE YOU CAN PEER DOWN AT THE CHURCH BELOW.

I think it has a special spirituality.

EAST

THE EAST IS THE MOST DIFFICULT REGION TO ACCESS. THIS IS TRUE NOT ONLY FOR ME AS A FOREIGNER, BUT ALSO FOR SERBS. EVEN IF YOU IGNORE LOGISTICAL CHALLENGES (NOTORIOUSLY BAD ROADS, IRREGULAR BUS CONNECTIONS, ETC), THE EAST DOES NOT SHARE ITS SECRETS READILY. MAYBE IT'S BECAUSE THERE ARE FEW OUTSIDE VISITORS, OR MAYBE THE CULTURE IS INTRINSICALLY MORE PRIVATE & ENIGMATIC. BUT IF YOU PERSEVERE, YOU WILL BE REWARDED: FROM VLACH MYSTICISM TO SURREAL VIEWS OF THE IRON GATES, THE EAST IS FULL OF MYSTERIES TO BE DISCOVERED.

KNJAŽEVAC

A VEHICULAR VANTAGE POINT:

↗ **FREZA** TRACTOR (factory is now closed, but the tractors remain)

SO PREVALENT, KNJAŽEVAC USED TO BE CALLED "GRAD MALIH TRAKTORA," OR "TOWN OF SMALL TRACTORS"

PONY BIKE

STRANGE SQUAT THINGS RIDDEN BY MANY-A FULLGROWN MAN. (made by same company that makes the TOMOS bike!)

knjazevac flavors

CHERRY BLOW-OUT!
cherry cake
washed down by
VISNJICA i.e. cherry
wine

ENJOYED AT THE JOVIĆ FAMILY WINERY. THIS PART OF SERBIA IS FAMOUS FOR ITS WINES (VRANAC IS MY FAVORITE)

TRKANICA
salad, a
local specialty
made of leeks, dried peppers, oil & salt

MANY MORE DISHES LEARNED OF BUT —ALAS!— NOT TASTED.

DONJA KAMENICA
church, ✠ exterior

→ its bizarre, unique shape is a bit of a mystery

← built in the 14th century

inside, you can clamber up an impossibly steep & narrow half-ladder-half-stairs to an upper room (with more frescoes!) where monks could pray in private.

Donja Kamenica church, interior.

MY FAVORITE FRESCOES:

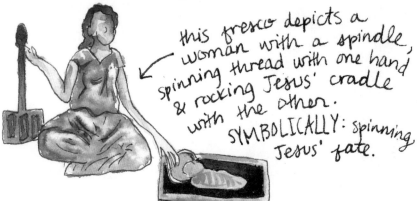

Jesus on the dinner table, representing sacrifice. usually, though, he's in ONE receptacle. This fresco is special because it shows the nature of Jesus' DOUBLE SACRIFICE

the plate is for BREAD (i.e. FLESH) while the bowl is for WINE (i.e. BLOOD) in the liturgy

this fresco depicts a woman with a spindle, spinning thread with one hand & rocking Jesus' cradle with the other.
SYMBOLICALLY: spinning Jesus' fate.

FAVORITE OBJECTS IN THE MUSEUM

the collection of **TWO-STRING SOCKS**, elaborately patterned knitwear made — as the name implies — with two strings

LARGE DOLLS dressed in detailed traditional costumes. made in the 1900s.

homeland museum, Knjazevac

generations in passing

ON THE STREET, KNJAŽEVAC

RGP building: state constructed it in the 1970s to house miners.

ringed by the remains of protective fortress walls

where the current nuns reside

THIS IS MY FAVORITE FRESCO *inside* Manasija Monastery (1407-1418). IT SHOWS GOD HOLDING HUMANKIND — *represented as swaddled infants* — IN HIS PALM. I LOVE <u>HANDS</u> IN GENERAL, so DEPICTIONS OF THE DIVINE HAND ARE PARTICULARLY MAGNETIC & ALLURING.

ROAD LIKE A PATCH-WORK QUILT.

BEEHIVES STACKED UP ON THE ROLLING HILLS.

THEY'RE SO JOLLY, IN THEIR BRIGHTLY-PAINTED WOODEN BOXES.

Lunch at Kapetan Misin Breg

chicken soup →

cabbage & lettuce in oil & vinegar

wine →

← proja

nettle fritters →

chicken & veal from the grill

← cheese

← mushrooms

marinated red potatoes

medovača →

vanilice for dessert →

AND FLOWERS STREWN EVERYWHERE

countryside bus stops

WOODEN SHELTER WITH — IF YOU'RE LUCKY — A BENCH INSIDE. OTHER ITERATIONS INCLUDE JUST A BENCH, OR EVEN JUST A GENERALLY KNOWN PIECE OF ROAD.

MAJDANPEK

a mining town: gaping pit surrounded by ominous, gargantuan apartment buildings.

RAJKO'S CAVE

(POPULATION: 7,000)

PRERAST

IRON GATES

BUT — surrounded by great natural beauty, especially the rocky sort: Rajko's cave, Prerast, & the Iron Gates aren't far off

crnajka village

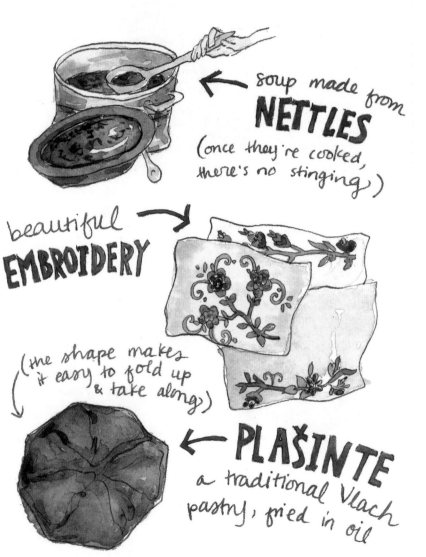

← soup made from **NETTLES** (once they're cooked, there's no stinging)

beautiful **EMBROIDERY** →

(the shape makes it easy to fold up & take along)

← **PLAŠINTE** a traditional Vlach pastry, fried in oil

Baba, fishing in the pickle jar with thick, soil-rimmed fingers.

two kinds of cheese: young & old

lump of kačamak in hand

kačamak

sliced pickles

A MODEST REPAST. DINNER IN A VLACH HOME NEAR BLIZNA VILLAGE.

KAČAMAK
IN BLIZNA VILLAGE

the pride of east serbian
dinner tables
everywhere

CORNMEAL COOKED IN WATER (LIKE GRITS!)

(optional: add cheese
and/or kajmak)

TOOLS OF THE TRADE:

blunt wood
knife for serving

wood
cutting
board

DRND, tool
for slicing

(it's rotated
between the
palms)

for
stirring
flour + water:
ČURKALO or **KAČAMALO**

Eastern Serbia's special cuisine — a sampling:

A VARIETY OF STINGING NETTLE DISHES (of course, no stinging once cooked!)

→ nettle pite

nettle fritters, battered & fried

nettle soup (my favorite!) →

VLAŠKA MUCKALICA

a rich Vlach stew of wild game (pig & deer) onions, mushrooms, etc

KAČAMAK, always kačamak

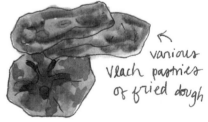

← various Vlach pastries of fried dough

↑ scallions on the side

lunch in Miroč

a traditional welcome from Staniša's four <u>ADORABLE</u> grandchildren:

AS A GUEST, YOU FOLLOW THESE STEPS:

STEP 1: tear off some bread
STEP 2: dip in salt
STEP 3: eat salty bread. optional: take more bread, dip in honey
STEP 4: take a glass of rakija

PIMNICE:

- CLUSTERS OF STONE WINE CELLARS PARTICULAR TO THIS
- REGION, BUILT STARTING IN THE 18TH CENTURY.

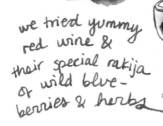

 ← in **ROGLJEVO,** the eccentric proprietor had loooong thumb-nails & a cellar converted into a museum of curiosities. (also, a mammoth skeleton in a shed).

we tried yummy red wine & their special rakija of wild blue-berries & herbs

in **RAJAC,** the Tamjanika white wine was the star, as well as the moody Beli Breg cemetery, whose 19th century gravestons are covered in linear designs & mystical symbols

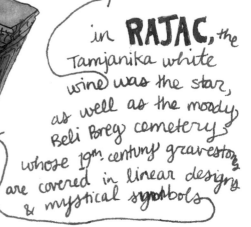

144

two worlds under one roof.

EVENING IN DONJI MILANOVAC

THE FIRST ROOM IN THE CAFÉ IS FILLED EXCLUSIVELY WITH SILENTLY SMOKING OLD MEN PLAYING DOMINOES; THEN YOU PASS INTO A SECOND ROOM FILLED WITH ONLY YOUNG PEOPLE, DRINKING & TALKING & PLAYING POOL.

145

NEGOTIN

← ornately carved gravestones (mostly from the 19th century) in the yard of the old church

Negotin is proud to be the birthplace of famous composer STEVAN STOJANOVIĆ MOKRANJAC. His house is now a lovely little museum. →

Neyotin handicrafts

called
ЗАНАРТ
or "ZANART"

floral motifs are classic

THERE'S A LOVELY SHOP WHERE WOMEN MAKE and SELL THEIR ETNO-STYLE WARES. COULDN'T SAY NO TO THESE JOLLY GLOVES.

SHE SITS
COMPLETELY
SURROUNDED BY
ICONS

baba Desanka

she told my fortune with dried corn kernels & a piece of thread from my sweater. baba desanka is a highly respected practitioner of Vlach magic.

СУСРЕТИ СЕЛА 2015

ACTS INCLUDE: *showcasing traditional activities & dress, acting out short plays (while consuming what was confirmed to be REAL rakija on stage), and*

→ *dancing* KOLO, *the traditional Serbian dance. Fancy footwork! each village has its own variation of steps*

"VILLAGE MEETINGS 2015": EACH SPRING, ABOUT 40 VILLAGES AROUND NEGOTIN FACE OFF IN A SERIES OF VIBRANT COMPETITIONS OF CREATIVE FOLK TRADITIONS. I SAW A GREAT SHOW IN SIKOLE.

unexpected treasures

in ŠTUBIK

we stopped for a coffee at Žika's sister's house. Turns out this tiny, ramshackle village was formerly the seat of a number of great empires throughout history. The people may forget, but the earth remembers!

WITH RED OVERALLS AND A HANDY METAL DETECTOR, SAŠA UNCOVERS TREASURES IN HIS SPARE TIME.

Saša showing how the job is done

collection includes:

ROMAN COINS

ROMAN JEWELRY

OTTOMAN COINS

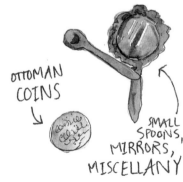

SMALL SPOONS, MIRRORS, MISCELLANY

Baba Jovanka

ONE OF THE MOST FAMOUS PRACTITIONERS OF VLACH MAGIC. WHEN WE ARRIVED AT HER HOUSE IN JABUKOVAC, A VILLAGE NEAR NEGOTIN, WE HAD TO WAIT WHILE SHE WORKED WITH A FOUR-YEAR-OLD BOY WHOSE WORRIED PARENTS BROUGHT HIM BECAUSE HE WON'T SPEAK. BABA JOVANKA TOLD US SHE GOT HER POWERS AS A YOUNG GIRL WHEN SHE WAS STRUCK BY LIGHTNING WHILE TENDING SHEEP. WHEN SHE CAME TO, SHE SAW HER GUIDING SPIRITS IN THE FORM OF THREE BEAUTIFUL LADIES. THEY'VE BEEN WITH HER EVER SINCE.

Jovanka told my fortune with cards

151

the famous
PIROT KILIM

I got a small kilim with the "KUVERI" (SUITCASES) pattern. It protects the traveler. I love the idea of talismans; Pirot kilims have a lexicon of over 200 symbols!

the suitcases are full — not of material, but of experience

the symbol in the middle represents the traveler, and the small white dots on radiating arms are all-seeing eyes for protection.

PRE-WWII, THERE WERE 5,000 WOMEN USING THE FIVE-CENTURIES-OLD WEAVING TECHNIQUE. NOW, ONLY ABOUT 20 REMAIN. IT'S AN EXTREMELY TIME-CONSUMING CRAFT: 80cm² TAKES ONE WOMAN 22 DAYS TO WEAVE IF SHE WORKS 8 HOURS PER DAY. LEARNING TO WEAVE IS A FIVE-YEAR PROCESS

POGANOVO MONASTERY

EXCELLENTLY-PRESERVED FRESCOES (15TH CENTURY).
SINCE I HAVE A "THING" FOR HANDS, I'M PARTIAL TO **THIS ONE**

the hands of god, crowning two saints with glory

BYZANTINE PATTERNING

A STUNNING 14TH-CENTURY CHURCH. TECHNICALLY, IT'S NAMED "ST JOHN THE THEOLOGIAN," BUT PEOPLE COLLOQUIALLY CALL IT AFTER THE NEARBY VILLAGE, WHICH IS UNFORTUNATE SEEING AS "POGAN" MEANS "FILTHY."

153

PIROT

LJUTENICA
a "spicy" salad — but only by serbian standards

(leeks, peppers, etc)

← **RECELJ**
a dessert made of pumpkin boiled in sweet red wine

PEGLANA →
unlike other Serbian meats, NO PORK ALLOWED — only lean sheep, goat, donkey, etc. Names means "IRONED", because it's rolled flat in preparation.

(horseshoe-shaped for good luck!)

← **KAČKAVALJ**
cheese

THE TOWN IS FAMOUS FOR ITS TEXTILES (KILIM CARPETS) AND FOR BEING THE BRUNT OF EVERY SERBIAN JOKE ABOUT STINGY PEOPLE (AT THIS POINT, BASED ON TRADITION, NOT REALITY!). BUT LET'S START WITH ITS FOOD...

kačkavalj cheese

A PIROT SPECIALTY. I GOT TO SEE THE SCHOOL/FACTORY WHERE THE MAGIC HAPPENS, STEP BY MILKY STEP!

START →

milk (70% cow, 30% sheep) it pasteurized in this contraption. FUN FACT: milk comes from 500 local cows each day. 10-12 liters of milk yields 1 kg of cheese.

cheese, gummy & stretchable from the heat, is kneaded & folded & salted

then placed in circular metal forms

cheese curds are sliced into thin, porous strips, and then...

finally, it's left to age (7 months to 2 years) with salt added periodically. a yummy **END**.

put in the boiling water

...loaded into a basket made of hazelnut wood (which has special elastic qualities that prevent it from breaking when submerged in boiling water)

155

THE TOWN WAS BUILT & FLUORISHED AROUND THE
COPPER MINE — BUT IT ALSO DISINTEGRATED WITH
IT. TODAY, BOR IS A HUGE TOXIC GASH IN THE EARTH
SURROUNDED BY SOCIALIST APARTMENT BLOCKS.

Ravanica

tucked snug & sound
into the lush green hills.

BUILT IN THE 14TH CENTURY. MORAVA SCHOOL STYLE.

West

WESTERN SERBIA IS REGION OF **EXTRAORDINARY** NATURAL BEAUTY, HOME TO TWO FAMOUS MOUNTAINS, NUMEROUS RIVERS, AND PLENTY OF GORGES & CAVES. IT'S ALSO A REGION KNOWN FOR ITS **PRIDE**. I WAS WARNED ABOUT THIS PRIDE BEFORE I VISITED, SO IN A CONVERSATION WITH ONE OF MY WESTERN HOSTS, I ASKED: "DID YOU KNOW THAT MANY SERBS THINK YOU ARE FULL OF **PRIDE & ARROGANCE?**" MY HOST WAS NOT OFFENDED IN THE LEAST. HE REPLIED: "WELL, YES, BUT WITH ALL **THIS**" — HE GESTURED WIDELY WITH HIS ARMS — "HOW COULD WE _NOT_ HAVE PRIDE?" IT WAS, I MUST SAY, THE PERFECT RESPONSE.

VALJEVO

statues commemorating Serb warriors killed in uprisings against the Ottomans

Statue of famous Serbian poet DESANKA MAKSIMOVIĆ, who was born here

NENADOVIĆ TOWER, built 1813

TEŠNJAR, picturesque street in the city center, 18th-19th century, Oriental style

IN A NUTSHELL

COOKIN' THE CABBAGE
[PRE-ČVARCI FESTIVAL PREPARATIONS]

the cabbage simmers away all night in huge iron pots

a very large man in a VERY small shirt presides over the laborious process, regularly feeding the fires & stirring the pots.

THE UBIQUITOUS
TOMOS BIKE

(TITO OPENED THE FIRST FACTORY IN 1959 IN
THE FORMER YUGOSLAVIA, TODAY SLOVENIA)

commonly seen puttering
around smaller towns,
emitting an earsplitting din.

on the street, VALJEVO

traditional Serbian hat called ŠAJKAČA, seen quite often around town

I love that the lamps are all adorned with potted plants

ROBAJE

VILLAGE POPULATION: APPROXIMATELY 300.

THIS IS WHERE JOVANA'S GRANDPARENTS LIVED + WORKED ALL THEIR LIVES. IT'S WHERE HER FATHER WAS BORN + RAISED — AS WAS JOVANA UNTIL SHE WAS 7, WHEN THE FAMILY MOVED TO NEARBY VALJEVO.

— built 1964 on the site of an older house

built in 1970s

↑ JOVANA, HER SISTER & HER PARENTS LIVED HERE IN THE "BIG HOUSE" (THREE ROOMS). TODAY IT'S EMPTY.

↑ JOVANA'S GRAND-MOTHER STILL LIVES HERE IN THE "SMALL HOUSE" (ONE ROOM + BATHROOM).

"THE SMALL HOUSE," *interior*

Baba sleeps here

when Deda was alive, he slept here

bathroom this way

← door to enter/exit

ALL·IN·ONE KITCHEN + LIVING ROOM + DINING ROOM + BEDROOM

Baka Bosiljka

IS A PROPER SERBIAN GRANNY. SHE GIVES US MANY KISSES IN THE HAIR, AS GRANNIES ARE WONT TO DO. SHE RECALLS HOW, ALL HER LIFE, SHE WOULD WALK THE TWO HOURS TO THE VALJEVO MARKET WITH A 30-KILO (66-POUND) SACK OF PEARS ON HER BACK. SHE DID THIS TWICE A WEEK. TODAY, SHE TENDS HER GOATS AND CHICKENS; GVOZDEN — JOVANA'S DAD, BAKA BOSILJKA'S SON — NOW HARVESTS THE PLUM & CHERRY TREES AS HIS FULL-TIME JOB.

THE CLASSIC VILLAGE SHOES
PIROĆANKE

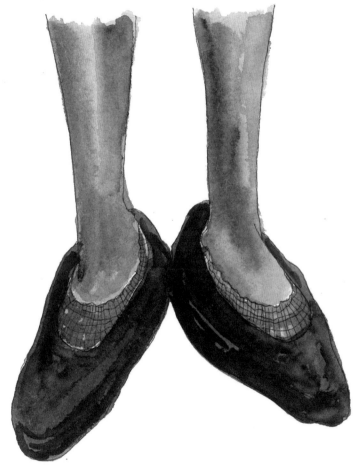

they're rubber — sturdy, functional,
comfortable — part boot, part slipper.
worn by men & women alike.

plums for rakija are held in these enormous barrels. There are maybe 10 in all, and each barrel holds 1.5 tons. The barrels only represent one tenth of the total plums produced on the family land!

(most barrels are plastic, but the wooden ones are over 100 years old).

PLUMS FERMENT FOR A COUPLE MONTHS. THEN IT'S TIME FOR THE DISTILLER:

fermented plums go here

the hot vapors are collected here in the KAPAK, or domed lid

wood is added here to keep the fire going!

hot vapors travel through this pipe & then to the KONDENZATOR (condenser), where they cool.

the stuff that comes out here is rakija! But you have to put it through the distiller again to get the alcohol content right.

RAKIJA PRODUCTION WITH TATA GVOZDEN.

Tata Gvozden holding a "NATEGA," a dried gourd used to transfer rakija

VILLAGE HANDS: *dexterous,* STRONG + PROFICIENT.

FINGERS THICK + SOLID, SKIN TOUGH, NAILS RINGED WITH SOIL — A LIFETIME OF WORKING THE EARTH, TENDING LIVESTOCK, RAISING A FAMILY. HANDS OF FORTITUDE.

Baka Bosiljka holding a plate of freshly-roasted pork

IN EVERY CELLAR OR PANTRY: STORES FOR WINTER

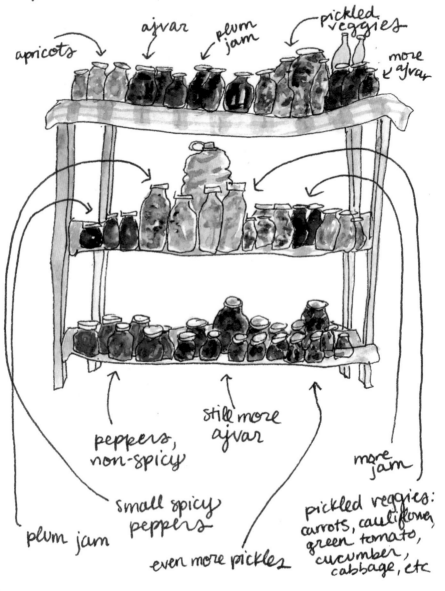

apricots

ajvar

plum jam

pickled veggies

more ajvar

peppers, non-spicy

still more ajvar

more jam

plum jam

small spicy peppers

even more pickles

pickled reggies: carrots, cauliflower, green tomato, cucumber, cabbage, etc

IN SERBIA, YOU MAKE SPECIAL OCCASIONS SPECIAL BY
Roasting a Pig

THANKS TO GVOZDEN FOR EXHIBITING & EXPLAINING THE PROCESS.

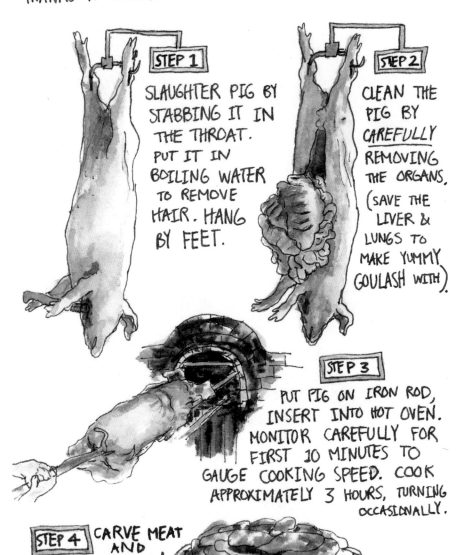

STEP 1

SLAUGHTER PIG BY STABBING IT IN THE THROAT. PUT IT IN BOILING WATER TO REMOVE HAIR. HANG BY FEET.

STEP 2

CLEAN THE PIG BY CAREFULLY REMOVING THE ORGANS. (SAVE THE LIVER & LUNGS TO MAKE YUMMY GOULASH WITH)

STEP 3

PUT PIG ON IRON ROD, INSERT INTO HOT OVEN. MONITOR CAREFULLY FOR FIRST 10 MINUTES TO GAUGE COOKING SPEED. COOK APPROXIMATELY 3 HOURS, TURNING OCCASIONALLY.

STEP 4 CARVE MEAT AND ENJOY!

pustinja monastery

the spectacular frescoes were painted in 1622. The one of St John the Baptist is famous, considered one of the most beautiful examples of medieval Serbian art.

NEW PART OF CHURCH—BUILT 1848

OLD PART OF CHURCH — BUILT 1622 ON SITE OF _MUCH_ OLDER CHURCH

as always, I visually "collect" the founder's composition. Original fresco painted in 1622.

IT WAS, AFTER ALL, JOVANA WHO
GAVE ME THE OPPORTUNITY TO SEE
PUSTINJA, DRIVING THE WINDING
ROADS TO ITS SECLUDED LOCATION.

RUSTIC & VERY STURDY FENCE
(TARABA)

sticks are woven together when they are young, malleable green saplings, then they harden into shape with age.

bunches of benches

flat cap

knit vest

piročanke shoes

VALJEVO, SERBIA

VIEW FROM THE CASTLE.

little red-roofed houses spattering the rolling hills, punctuated by socialist-architecture giants jutting out, agressive & discordant, from the cityscape.

komplet lepinja

"lepinja" bread filled with eggs & kajmak, drizzled with lamb or pork fat

THE BE-ALL-END-ALL, HEART-ATTACK-INDUCING CULINARY PRIDE OF UŽICE. OTHER MORE GENERAL WESTERN SPECIALTIES INCLUDE:

PRŠUTA
(prosciutto)

KAJMAK

SIR (cheese)

PORK AND LAMB PEČENJE
(roasted on a spit)

lunch on Tara mountain

← bread rolls

← thick, salty veal soup

ŠOPSKA salad: tomato, cucumber, and melt-in-your-mouth cheese

veal medallions in sauce with mushrooms; potatoes & carrots on the side

← house-specialty PALAČINKE (crêpes) for dessert: filled with walnuts & covered in sweet white wine foam

MY HOST ASKED IF I KNEW THE 3 MOST IMPORTANT THINGS IN THE WEST. I admitted I did not. HE SAID "IT'S EASY: BREAKFAST, LUNCH & DINNER!

traditional western architecture

(from the late 19th and early 20th centuries)

WOODEN HOUSES IN SIROGOJNO

ST MARK'S CHURCH IN UŽICE

WOODEN STRUCTURES WITH A SPECIFIC ANGULAR, POINTY-ROOFED LOOK. LATER (1960s & 70s) THE SOCIALIST ARCHITECTS RIFFED OFF THE SHAPES BUT UTILIZED NEW MATERIALS AND BUILT ON A NEW (HUGE) SCALE.

HOTEL ZELENKADA, ZLATIBOR

HOTEL OMORIKA, TARA

ZLAKUSA VILLAGE

perhaps most famous for its pottery production

GREAT ATTENTION TO PRESERVING VILLAGE TRADITION

look out for the signature "Z" (for "Zlakusa") which indicates authenticity

coat rack made of animal hooves

FROM THE FABULOUS **ETNO PARK** **TERZICA AVLIJA**

in the old schoolhouse: the original calculator!

and HUNDREDS of other antique artifacts that span centuries

dolls

Mokra Gora & Bajina Bašta

ŠARGAN EIGHT →

train in Mokra Gora.
The scenic tracks
make a figure 8

between Mokra Gora & Bajina
Bašta, you pass through
KREMNA VILLAGE,
where the famous
Tarabić prophesiers
lived & died

THE RIVER HOUSE

in Bajina Bašta. Perched
precariously on a
rock smack-dab in
the middle of the
river Drina

ČAČAK

HOTEL BEOGRAD, an excellent example of secessionist/art nouveau architecture in Serbia — and quite similar to Hotel Moskva in Belgrade

← small but superb **MUSEUM** with artifacts ranging from pre-history to WWII

(and some beautiful natural surroundings!)

holy water

FOLKS BELIEVE DEEPLY IN THE SPECIAL HEALING POWERS OF CERTAIN WATERS, ESPECIALLY THOSE NEAR CHURCHES. ALEKSANDAR TOOK A WHOLE BIG BOTTLE OF THE WATER KNOWN PARTICULARLY FOR HEALING EYES, BECAUSE HE HAS AN EYE DISEASE HE HOPES TO CURE.

you use the roper to hoist up the bucket of water from the well

(I HOPE IT WORKS!)

OVČAR · KABLAR GORGE

KABLAR mountain ↓

OVČAR mountain ←

SRETENJE

SVETA TROJICA

PREOBRAŽENJE

KAĐENICA CAVE

VAZNESENJE

VAVEDENJE

SVETI ILIJA

ST SAVA HERMITAGE

BLAGOVEŠTENJE

USPENJE

JOVANJE

NIKOLJE

WEST MORAVA RIVER

OFTEN CALLED "HOLY MOUNTAN" OR "THE SERBIAN MOUNT ATHOS" BECAUSE OF THE 12 HOLY PLACES CONCENTRATED THERE. MOST SPRUNG UP IN THE 15TH + 16TH CENTURIES DURING OTTOMAN REIGN.

holy nooks & crannies

outside **ST NICHOLAS CHURCH** there's a special tree. People circle it, pray, and press coins into the bark.

in Ovčar-Kablar gorge

natural stone water basin at **ST SAVA HERMITAGE.** spot for prayer.

people have left: icons, vessels for gathering water, coins.

in **BLAGOVEŠTENJE** church: an alcove carved into the wall. contains a crocheted cross, icons, an apple in a basket.

St Nicholas (Nikolje) monastery

FRESCOES FROM THE 16ᵀᴴ + 17ᵀᴴ CENTURIES →

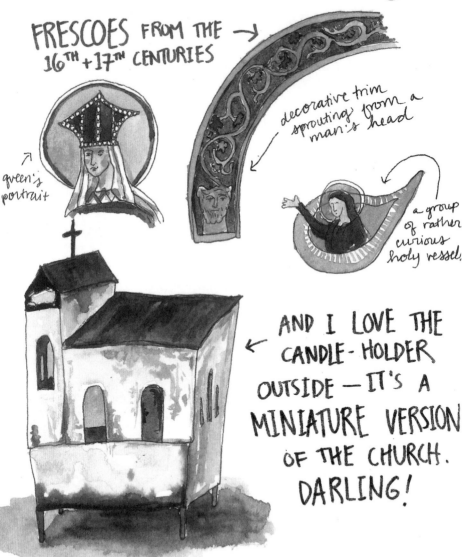

↗ queen's portrait

decorative trim sprouting from a man's head

a group of rather curious holy vessel,

← AND I LOVE THE CANDLE-HOLDER OUTSIDE — IT'S A **MINIATURE VERSION** OF THE CHURCH. **DARLING!**

KRAJPUTAŠI

roadside memorials specific to the
West, featuring stylized, stocky figures

the name
literally
means
"ROADSIDE"

THESE MEMORIALS, MOSTLY FROM THE EARLY 20TH CENTURY,
WERE ERECTED BY FAMILY MEMBERS WHO WANTED TO
COMMEMORATE A SOLDIER WHO DIED FAR FROM HOME.
SINCE BODIES WERE NOT RETURNED, KRAJPUTAŠI
SERVED AS BOTH GRAVE AND TRIBUTE TO SERVICE

Baka Jakova

THE MATRIARCH OF THE LJUBOJEVIĆ FAMILY — THE FAMILY THAT REVIVED & CURRENTLY RUNS THE SIROGOJNO COMPANY — STILL KNITS AT 93 YEARS OLD. GLOVES ARE HER SPECIALTY, KNOWN TO BE DIFFICULT BECAUSE YOU HAVE TO KNIT EACH FINGER SEPARATELY. THERE'S ALSO A GREAT STORY ABOUT HER: WHEN THE BULGARIAN ARMY CAME TO THE VILLAGE IN WWII, THEY WERE TAKING ALL THE SHEEP. JAKOVA BRAVELY IMPLORED THE SOLDIERS TO LET HER KEEP ONE SHEEP. THEY AGREED — SHE PROMPTLY GRABBED THE ONE WITH THE BELL AROUND ITS NECK & STARTED RUNNING — THE REST OF THE FLOCK FOLLOWED!

Sirogojno,
AKA A SWEATER HEAVEN

HUNDREDS
OF ORNATE
PATTERNS

this small village
in Western Serbia is
famous for its sweater
production. The visionary
business initiative has
employed women in the
region since the 1960s.

THE LARGEST CITY IN **CENTRAL SERBIA**, OR **ŠUMADIJA**. IT PRIDES ITSELF ON ITS *FIRSTS:*

first **HIGH SCHOOL** (or "GYMNASIUM") in the newly independent Serbian state

where the first Serbian **CONSTITUTION** was drafted & signed →

Serbia's first **THEATER**, founded in 1835.

KRAGUJEVAC
the first capital city in modern Serbia!

MUSEUM "21 OKTOBAR"

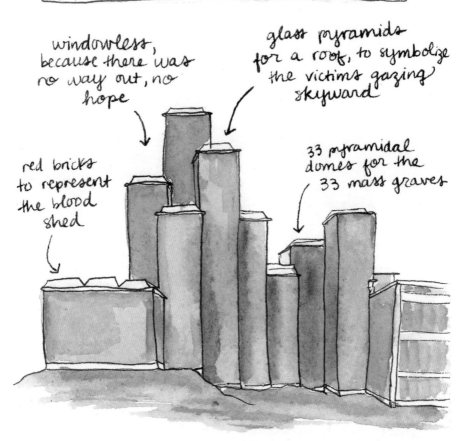

windowless, because there was no way out, no hope

glass pyramids for a roof, to symbolize the victims gazing skyward

red bricks to represent the blood shed

33 pyramidal domes for the 33 mass graves

MUCH OF KRAGUJEVAC'S IDENTITY IS DEFINED BY THE TRAGEDIES THAT TRANSPIRED THERE IN WWII, MOST NOTABLY THE MASSACRE OF 7,000 MALE CITIZENS — INCLUDING A CLASS OF HIGH SCHOOL BOYS — ON OCTOBER 21, 1941.

Kafana Jugoslavija

if you like the music,
you put some money
into the folds of the accordian

since it was Thursday night, they
had traditional music as entertainment

THE WHOLE INTERIOR IS PAINTED LIKE THE
YUGOSLAVIAN FLAG, SO IT'S REALLY AN
ALL-ENCOMPASSING, IMMERSIVE EXPERIENCE.

(and don't forget the
bust of Tito at the entrance!)

spicy green pepper in oil

dunja (quince) rakija

a block of feta cheese

svad-barski kupus, or WEDDING CABBAGE: cabbage & meats, simmered to perfection in great big pots for hours & hours.

bread fried in butter, garlic, & salts/spices

SUSTENANCE AT ITS FINEST AT KAFANA JUGOSLAVIJA.

THE "OLD" & "NEW" CHURCHES IN KRAGUJEVAC.

"OLD" built in 1818. "NEW" built from 1869-84.

THE GREEN CHAIRS
IN THE OLD CHURCH

smaller one for the priest

bigger one for Prince Miloš Obrenović (who built the church in 1818).

that GREEN! vivid & rich

THERE IS SOMETHING VERY INTIMATE ABOUT A CHAIR, ESPECIALLY ONE MADE FOR A PARTICULAR PERSON — I CAN JUST _SEE_ PRINCE MILOŠ OBRENOVIĆ PERCHED THERE.

public TRANSPORT PORTRAITS

ONE
šajkača cap →

THREE
canes (??!?)

TWO
bags

mysterious numbers!
exiting the bus,
kragujevac to Belgrade.

THE SHOE COBBLER'S WINDOW: SQUAT
GNOME FIGURINES, HALF-DEAD PLANTS,
SHOELACES, SMALL OPANCI, MISCELLANY.

on the street,
Kragujevac

BIOGRAPHY

EMMA FICK WAS BORN IN 1991 IN COVINGTON, LOUISIANA IN THE USA. SHE RECEIVED HER BA IN ENGLISH LITERATURE FROM THE UNIVERSITY OF ALABAMA IN TUSCALOOSA. SHE BEGAN ILLUSTRATING WHEN SHE MOVED TO SERBIA TO TEACH ENGLISH IN 2013, AND IS NOW SETTING OFF ON AN ADVENTURE (AKA CAREER) AS A TRAVEL ILLUSTRATOR. THIS IS HER FIRST BOOK. (SEE MORE AT WWW.EMMAFICK.COM)

CIP - Каталогизација у публикацији -
Народна библиотека Србије, Београд

741/744:929 Фик Е.

FICK, Emma, 1991-
Snippets of Serbia / illustrations [and texts] by Emma Fick. - Beograd :
Komshe, 2015 (Beograd : Publikum). - [200] str. : ilustr. ; 22 x 16 cm

Tiraž 1.000. - Biography: str. [199].

ISBN 978-86-86245-26-7

a) Фик, Ема (1991-) - Илустрације
COBISS.SR-ID 215584524